LINEN EMBROIDERY

Worked by Mrs. Cameron, Medstead, Hampshire

LINEN EMBROIDERY

Etta Campbell

London

B. T. BATSFORD LTD

ISBN 0 7134 6251 5

PRINTED AND BOUND IN GREAT BRITAIN BY
COURIER INTERNATIONAL LTD, TIPTREE, ESSEX
FOR THE PUBLISHERS
B. T. BATSFORD LTD
4 FITZHARDINGE STREET, LONDON, W1H 0AH

PREFACE

I have been encouraged to write this book by the fact that although many designs can be obtained which are suitable for Linen Embroidery, there appears very little in the way of technical help, other than that obtainable through Schools of Art or Technical Colleges. There are many needlewomen who are able to master stitches from embroidery books, but this is difficult for some people, and so I hope my notes and hints may be useful to those who are interested and anxious to work this most absorbing type of embroidery.

I should like to express my thanks for the help I have received from my students at the Winchester School of Art, as well as others whom I have had the privilege of teaching and who have so kindly undertaken the production of some of the worked models illustrated in the book; especially to Mrs. Cameron and Miss Lovell for lending their samplers, to Miss Dorothy Lewis who has so kindly and patiently corrected my proofs, and finally to Miss Sylvia Green for her clear and accurate reproductions of my diagrams.

Etta Campbell

Twyford,
Winchester, Hampshire
August 1957

CONTENTS

		Page
Preface		7
Introduction		11
	Transferring Design to Material	13
	Tension	13
	Fastening On and Off	14
	Hems	14
	Borders	15
	Double Running	16
	Stretching and Pressing the Finished Work	17
	Samplers	18
Books and Materials		20
Samplers		23, 25
1	Square Stitch	26
2	Square Stitch—variation	27
3	Square Diagonal with open spaces	28
4	Square Diagonal with two threads left	29
5	Square Diagonal with small squares	30
6	Square Diagonal with bars	31
7	Basket Stitch	32
8	Mosaic Stitch	33
9	Pulled Chevron	34
10	Reversed Diagonal	35
11	Square Diagonal with one thread left	36
12	Square Diagonal with thread left	37
13	Greek Cross Stitch	38
14	Greek Cross Stitch—variation	39
15	Single Raised Band	40
16	Double Raised Band	41
17	Solid Eyelet	42
18	Eyelet with Shadow Stitch Square	43
19	Single Eyelet Stitch	44
20	Three-sided Stitch	45
21	Pulled Satin Stitch—variation	46
22	Pulled Satin Stitch—variation	47

CONTENTS

		Page
23	Pulled Back Stitch	48
24	Festoon Stitch	49
25	Eyelet Stitch Filling	50
26	Rosette Stitch	51
27	Ringed Back Stitch	52
28	Ringed Back Stitch with box	53
29	Honeycomb Stitch	54
30	Lozenge Stitch - variation	55
31	Lozenge Stitch—variation	56
32	Braid Stitch over two threads	57
33	Wave Stitch	58
34	Wave Stitch—variation	59
35	Pulled Square	60
36	Pulled Square—variation	61
	Outlines for Using with Pulled Fillings	62–3
	Borders	64–5
	Geometrical Satin Stitch	66–7
	Double Running or Holbein Stitch	68–9
	Index	71

LINEN EMBROIDERY

I do not feel quite certain that *Linen Embroidery* is the correct title for this book. It is possible that to many needlewomen Richelieu, Reticella and Broderie Anglaise come under this heading, whereas I am concerned only with linen worked by the thread of the material—pulled work, double running and geometrical satin stitch. In mentioning names, I should like to quote from *Art in Needlework* by Lewis F. Day, published by Batsford in 1900, to show that over fifty years ago the same feeling existed then, as today, about the names of stitches, and if some of mine are different, and some have no names at all, I hope I may be forgiven for adding to the confusion.

"The difficulty of discussing stitches", wrote Lewis F. Day, "is greatly increased by the haphazard way in which they are commonly named. A stitch is called Greek, Spanish, Mexican, according to the Country whence came the work in which someone first found it. Each names it after his or her individual discovery or calls it, perhaps vaguely, Oriental, and so we have a number of names for the same stitch; names which to different people often stand for quite different stitches. When this confusion is complicated by the invention of a new name for every conceivable combination of thread stitches or for the slightest variation upon an old stitch, and even for a stitch worked from left to right instead of from right to left, or for a stitch worked rather larger than usual, the task of reducing them to order seems almost hopeless."

I should like to add to Mr. Day's wise remarks on this difficult question of names of stitches, that I have always understood that there are really only five basic stitches in Needlework—Running, Oversewing, Buttonholing, Interlacing and Knotting, although, of course, there are literally hundreds of combinations and variations.

To write on embroidery and to embark on the subject of counting the threads of the material may not sound very inspiring, and yet, to many embroideresses, this pulled and counted work proves a most enthralling type of needlework. It entails concentration as well as skill and patience, and if, in addition, there is an eye for design and colour, very beautiful pieces of embroidery can be produced. After very little experience a worker will find that counting the threads becomes almost mechanical. I say almost, because even to the most expert embroideress, there will inevitably be the need for accuracy, and it is this need which gives the work the power to absorb the mind. I firmly believe that an hour a day at this type of work will act as a tonic to tired nerves and brains, as well as giving an added interest to everyday life.

I hope some of the following hints may not seem too trivial or elementary, but so often work is spoilt by untidy or careless finishings.

To start at the very beginning, material is important. This should always be linen, although there are today some substitutes which can be used, but, of course, these cannot be expected to give the same results. The type of linen must be left to the worker, who will consider the purpose of her embroidery. To use a fine scrim for a piece of work which will have hard wear, or a heavy linen for fine table mats, would be equally unsuitable. The size of the weave to suit the eye-sight must be considered, the threads to be used, the size and the colour. And last, but certainly not least, is the design. It is obvious that if an embroideress can design her own work she will produce a more individual and, probably, a better result, simply because the entire conception and execution will be her own work. But on the other hand, there are plenty of good designs to be obtained which will give more satisfaction than using a bad, or perhaps it is kinder to say, a less good design, simply because the worker produced it herself. Designs can be so easily altered and adapted, that there need be no fear of copying too slavishly. It is a pity that more use is not made of our beautiful traditional designs—quilting, the trade signs on the old smocks, and, of course, the Jacobean work; any of these will give wonderful ideas for free-hand designs, using the pulled stitches for fillings. Any free-hand design will give the worker more scope for her skill than the formal geometrical types. It will prove interesting and helpful to change the size of the stitches from the usual three threads to two, this giving the variety of light and shade which colour would produce. A heavy or a light stitch—a different size of thread—will also be found satisfactory.

The subject of colour for this work is a most controversial one and there are many embroideresses and others who are against it. In early days self colour was nearly always used, but today there is a great desire for colour, especially amongst our younger needlewomen, and I can see no reason why it should not be used. It will, of course, considerably alter the appearance of the work. Instead of the pulled holes being the main point, it will be the coloured threads which will be outstanding. To so many workers this embroidery is not only fascinating, but is soothing, peaceful and happy to work, and I believe that more would embark on it if colour were looked upon with more favour than it is at present.

There is no need to fear eyestrain if ordinary precautions are taken. Work in a good light, with the light coming over the left shoulder, never face the light. At the slightest feeling of strain, pause for a few minutes and then work at a different stitch, which will alter the focus and no harm will be done to your sight. In fact I have been told on good authority, that with reasonable care, this type of embroidery will strengthen the eyesight, and I have proved this to be true by some of my students.

TRANSFERRING DESIGN TO MATERIAL

There are various methods of applying a design on to the material.

1. The somewhat laborious pricking and pouncing is looked upon as the best. The design is drawn on to transfer paper, which is then pricked all round; with a soft rag make a firm ball over cotton wool; this is rubbed into a mixture of powdered chalk and charcoal and run over the pricked holes. Remove the drawing and with a fine paint-brush or pen go over the design.

2. Make a drawing on to transfer paper which should be pinned to the top of the work. Use a small piece of carbon paper, a piece that has been used is the best. Trace with an agate tracing pencil or a steel knitting needle, and place a piece of glass under the work; this will help to keep a clear, fine line which will be easy to completely cover in working. Care is needed not to press on the carbon paper or it may mark the material.

3. With some designs it is easy to cut out the design in thin card and draw round it.

4. The design can be drawn directly on to the work.

A free-hand design should have the fillings worked first, with an outline added. With a geometrical design, the outline is worked first.

TENSION

One of the most important details in pulled work is the tension of the stitches, and unless this is kept even and regular the whole effect will be spoilt. Use a hard linen thread; the size must depend on the material as well as the size of the stitch; use a short length of thread in the needle, which will enable the worker to give one pull to each stitch, and not a series of short tugs. Use a blunt-pointed tapestry needle, as fine as the thread will allow; it is a good idea constantly to move the thread in the eye of the needle as linen thread very soon wears rough and even changes colour which again will destroy the even appearance of the work. Another method of keeping a good tension is always to hold the work the way the stitches will travel. Do not work sideways, the pull will be uneven and unsatisfactory. Always work underneath the previous row, never above it. This will, of course, often mean fastening off and restarting, although sometimes it is possible to turn the work and travel underneath the previous row.

I wonder if I may add a word of warning here. Some workers "pat" each stitch as they finish it. If asked why they do it, they will often say they are quite ignorant of doing so. But linen threads are fragile and will soon show signs of wear if this trick, for I am sure it is just a trick, becomes a habit.

FASTENING ON AND OFF

Fastening on and off must be kept as neat and inconspicuous as possible, but do not let this be a worry to you. You will never do good work unless you are happy in the making, and are really enjoying it. The fastening on and off must show, but they need not spoil the work. In pulled work there will usually be three threads for a stitch. Unless there is no alternative, never start or end on a diagonal stitch. Bring the needle to the right side of the work, pick up two threads, go over them—this is called a "bind"—and pull the thread; pick up the third thread, bringing the needle back into the first stitch, and the thread will be quite secure. To fasten off, take the needle to the wrong side and run a few stitches into the work, taking care that at least one stitch picks up the material with a small backstitch.

HEMS

Hems are important. Sometimes the linen is not cut exactly by the threads, and so it is essential to be careful before beginning a hem. They should be kept narrow, but not so narrow that it becomes a roll; it should be quite flat. One thread is pulled out for hemstitching: $\frac{5}{8}$ of an inch for an ordinary linen, $\frac{3}{4}$ for a coarse one, will give a suitable size for the hem. Cut this thread about 2 inches from the corner; on two sides of the work, pull these two ends into the corner. When pulling out these threads bring them out sideways, not upwards; this will avoid a hole which when worked will always show. It is most necessary that the finished hemstitching should be clear and neat. Diagram 1 (p. 15) shows the first detail, Diagram 2 the first turn of the hem and the mitre in place for working. This mitred corner will give a much better result than the square finish. Diagrams 3 and 4 show the needle in place for hemstitching. The thread has been fastened on to the hem, three threads picked up and covered a second time, the needle is then taken at right angles into the hem, with a small stitch which should not be carried to the right side of the work. Pick up the next three threads and continue, leaving enough space to prepare the mitre. Diagram 5 shows the needle on the left-hand side; being taken between the fold of the hem to the point, it is then brought down on the right-hand side into the corner, with a small stitch to keep the ends of the mitre together and repeat (p. 27). The last hemstitch in the corner should always be over three threads. A linen thread is always the best for hems, which need a firm, even pull with each stitch. To help preserve this even appearance of the finished hem, it is advisable to be careful in pulling out the one thread. The best method is to cut this thread at short intervals, pull out about two or three

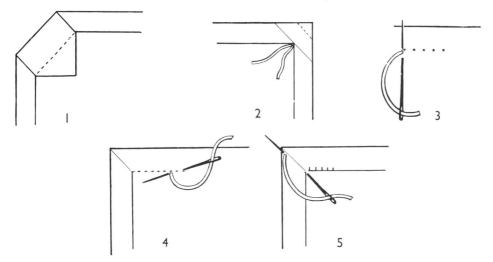

inches, and work. Do not pull the thread out for a longer space or the threads will move and the stitch in hemstitching will not be clear. If it is felt that this narrow hem is unsuitable for a large piece of work, add a border. Two or more rows of pulled satin stitch, with raised square stitch, leaving one thread un-covered, and repeat the pulled satin stitch, will give extra weight. These rows of pulled satin stitch with any of the pulled stitches between them will have the same effect. I do not advocate the decorated hems which are now being used, nor a wide hem. The charm of linen embroidery is its simplicity, and may I add its dignity, and with trimmings and edges added to a really even and well-worked hem, these details are apt to be lost.

BORDERS

In planning a border for a square piece of work, it must be remembered that in many linens there are more threads in the warp (selvedge) than in the weft, which means that it may not be possible to have exactly the same number of repeats of the design on all four sides of the work. Always make a good corner; it is advisable to work one corner and a couple of inches of the border, and then work the second corner. If the designs do not join quite accurately, it is

15

possible to adjust or to leave a small space in the centre of each side. It is most important that the corners should be well planned. If working a border across the work, with no corner, start in the centre of the work which, of course, will also be the centre of the design, working out to each side.

In planning a large piece of work, it will be a great help to run a fine coloured thread from the centre across to each side. The accurate centre of the work will be seen easily and much counting will be saved. It is, of course, of the utmost importance that this line of tacking should be absolutely accurate, and every stitch worked over the correct number of threads.

DOUBLE RUNNING, ALSO KNOWN AS HOLBEIN OR STROKE STITCH

This is one of the very early types of embroidery; there are examples of this stitch in existence now which were found in the ancient Egyptian tombs.

It is not a difficult stitch, but needs care and patience; when finished the work should look exactly alike on both sides.

The method of working is to find the "travelling" line in the design, which is worked on the first journey. Pick up three threads, needle over them and under the next three and so on. It is a matter of personal feeling whether the "offshoots" in the design are worked on the first or second journey. In the model and diagram the travelling line are the steps, and the flowers and hooks are the offshoots. For the return journey, when the uncovered stitches are worked, care must be taken to place the needle above the stitch to be worked and bring it out underneath, as shown in Diagram on p. 17. This will make an even line. Some workers find it easier to start the second journey in the same place as the first, travelling the same way. The other method is to reverse and travel the opposite way. The result will be the same, but I believe there is less chance of making any mistakes if the first method is adopted. The same stitch is used for the Black work fillings, except that it is not always perfect double running—the back will not always be exactly the same as the front.

On the usual Glenshee linen the D.M.C. coton perle on balls, Number 8 is a good thread to use. Do not use a stranded thread, because the finished effect should be a clear even line. Fastening on and off are the only real difficulties in this work to ensure that the back and front of the work should be exactly the same. There must be a slight thickening of the threads, but with neatness and care this should not spoil the work. In most designs there will be one or two straight stitches; and these should be used for starting and finishing. On the right side of the work darn over the stitch, under one thread, over the next and under the third; cover this stitch and leave a short end of the thread, which will be cut off after the second journey. To fasten off use the same method but on the wrong side of the work. If the design has more than one straight stitch fasten on or off over more than one stitch.

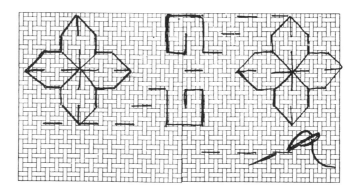

If a colour is being used it should be a clear strong one, not a pastel shade. More than one colour is often used when the design is a suitable one.

STRETCHING AND PRESSING THE FINISHED WORK

A most important part in embroidery is the stretching or pressing, and many pieces of work are spoilt by careless or over-pressing. The most satisfactory

17

method is to stretch the work, but this is not possible on work which is already hemmed, because in pinning out the straight edge of a hem will be spoilt.

Before pinning out the work it is advisable to tack a tape or some fine material all round to take the strain of the stretching. Place the work, face downwards, on to a piece of linen or damask, taking care to keep it perfectly straight. With rustless pins or drawing-pins, pin the work at short intervals all round. It will be easier if this pinning is started in the centre, from the top to the lower edge, and then from side to side. Care must be taken to keep the edges quite straight, or the result will be uneven. With a sponge or a piece of linen well dampen the work, taking care that the whole surface is wet, and leave to dry.

If it is decided to iron the work, place it face downwards on to a piece of linen over a soft material; flannel or blanket is ideal, as this soft surface will prevent the threads from being flattened. Over the work place a well-damped piece of linen. Take a very hot iron, press quickly over the damped linen, but do not iron until it is dry: just one quick pressing and hang up to dry. Never let the iron touch the embroidery, either on the right or wrong side.

The models have been worked on a coarse Glamis linen, in black D.M.C. coton perle, Number 8. It should be remembered that these materials give a different result from that expected in linen embroidery, usually worked with much finer materials and in self-coloured threads, which means that the holes made by the pulled stitches will show and not the threads. It was felt that the black thread on a coarse linen would enable the stitches to be seen more clearly, and copied, assisted by reference to the captions for each stitch. The models are nearly always worked over three threads, although it is sometimes necessary to use four. The numbers for each model serve to identify them on the sampler with its key. This sampler is worked on scrim, using black filoselle—sometimes with one strand, sometimes with two or even three, according to the size and type of stitch.

I do not consider it is necessary to use a frame for this type of embroidery, but, of course, if it is found to be a help, by all means use one.

SAMPLERS

I should advise all needlewomen to produce a sampler, not necessarily a finished piece of work, but something on which each stitch is worked when learnt, so that it is easy to make a selection of suitable stitches, instead of copying from a book. This type of sampler would then take the place of a note-book. A finished sampler is a most delightful piece of work, both from the point of view of its execution and also of its pictorial value. There are several types of samplers.

1. The sampler of stitches, worked without much planning, and, if preferred, in many colours and various types of threads.
2. The sampler of designs, borders, corners and small motifs, all very useful for reference when embarking on a large piece of work.
3. The pictorial sampler, portraying the story of the worker's life and interests. This does require a certain amount of design, but it can become a most fascinating piece of work.

But whichever type you choose, please add your name, the name of the place in which you live and the date.

The three samplers shown give some idea of what can be produced. Mrs. Cameron's work (Frontispiece) shows various types of linen embroidery, in designs adapted mostly from Miss L. F. Pesel's books. It is again on scrim and the stitchery is worked in filoselle, the greater part in black, with the number of threads varied to suit the stitches. Colours, red, blue and green, are used for the double running. The outlines on the three details at the top of the sampler are in cream, using satin stitch, with pale grey for the centre work. The double running detail in the centre is worked in nigger brown, with the cream satin stitch in the interlacing.

The two samplers of stitches worked in black, by the authoress, need no explanations (pp. 23, 25). They are the same stitches as the models and diagrams, but I hope they will show what this type of work should look like when worked with finer material than that used for the models.

I should like to think that this book may encourage some needlewomen to work a sampler, so that future generations will know that even in these days of restlessness and stress, and the ever-increasing desire for machine work, some of us still enjoyed producing fine, and, as far as our capabilities allowed, really beautiful handwork.

"A thing of beauty is a joy for ever."

BOOKS

Historical Designs for Embroidery. Miss L. F. Pesel. Batsford.
Dictionary of Stitches. Mary Thomas. Hodder and Stoughton.
Drawn Fabric. Kate Lofthouse. Pitman.
Linen Embroideries. Etta Campbell. Pitman.
Samplers and Stitches. Mrs. Christie. Batsford.
Encyclopedia of Needlework. D.M.C.
Embroidery. Quarterly journal of the Embroiderers Guild.

LINENS

Bisso. Glamis. Glenshee. Scrim. Italian.	Plummer, Ltd., High Street, Winchester.
Glamis, Glenshee, Scrim.	Miss M. Croft, Black Swan Buildings, Winchester.
Glenshee, Glamis (also in colours) Scrim white and colours. Bisso	Mrs. Seward, 3 Clarence Road, Hunstanton, Norfolk.

THREADS

Knox L.C. white and colours C.B. colours.	Miss M. Croft.
D.M.C. Knox. C.B. threads. Also all D.M.C. publications. Tapestry needles.	Mrs. Seward.
Transfers	The Embroiderers Guild, 56, Queen Anne Street, London, W.1.

MATERIALS

LINENS

Glenshee, in white, natural and in certain colours, is an even weave and is easy to work on and is a very usual size in weave. For heavier work Glamis is a coarser weave. This can also be obtained in colours. Scrim, also known as Lauder gauze, is a fine material but is clear and easy to work. It can be obtained in white or natural and also in a few colours. The Italian linen is rather a heavy make, with a close weave. This can only be had in white. The Bisso linen is very fine, in white or natural. All these materials are 50–54 inches wide.

THREADS

C.B. and D.M.C. threads can be obtained in a very good range of colours. Coton perle on balls, No. 8 is a very useful size for most work, or if a finer thread is needed No. 12. These threads would be for Double running, or for any stitches where colour is needed. Stranded cotton or filoselle may also be used, but the best result will be obtained when using a hard linen thread. Knox L.C. in skeins, from numbers 20 to 70 in white and various shades of natural, and also in colours, are easy to work. The same makers have a floss thread, also in colours, for using for geometrical satin stitch. D.M.C. make a very fine linen thread No. 270 in white and natural for using on the Bisso linen.

NEEDLES

Use tapestry needles, size 26 for fine work. 22–24 for coarser linen.

KEY TO SAMPLER

1. Pulled back stitch

2. Pulled chevron

3. Diagonal design

4. Pulled square

5. Square diagonal variety 4

6. Ringed back stitch

7. Honeycomb

8. Raised square stitch and pulled overcast

9. Satin stitch

10. Basket stitch

11. Eyelet

12. Reversed diagonal

13. Square diagonal variety 2

14. Square diagonal variety 1

15. Greek cross

16. Honeycomb variety

17. Satin stitch

18. Pulled back stitch

19. Double running

20. Ringed back stitch variety

21. Ringed back stitch raised square

22. Greek cross variety

23. Eyelet variety.

24. Satin stitch pulled centre

25. Square diagonal variety 3

26. Satin stitch border

27. Square diagonal with loop stitch

30. Satin stitch pulled

28. Raised band

29. Reversed diagonal pulled centre

31. Satin stitch border

33. Wave stitch

34. Satin stitch

35. Damask filling

32. Pulled square variety

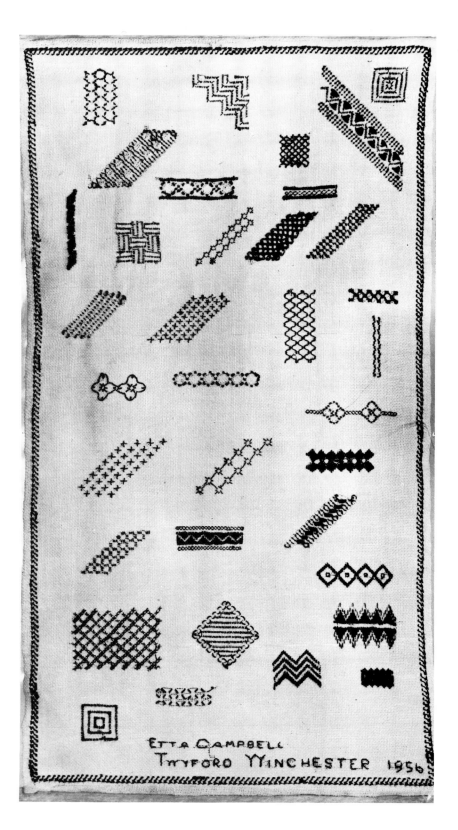

ETTA CAMPBELL
TWYFORD WINCHESTER 1956

KEY TO SAMPLER

36. Rosette

37. Festoon

38. Lozenge

39. Lozenge variety

40. Pulled satin stitch

41. Braid stitch

42. Pulled satin stitch with Greek Cross

43. Pulled satin stitch

44. Pulled satin with raised square stitches

45. Pulled satin and square stitches

46. Mosaic

47. Pulled satin stitch

48. Single raised band

49. Square diagonal with small squares

50. Eyelet.

51. Three-sided stitch

52. Eyelet with shadow stitch

53. Solid eyelet

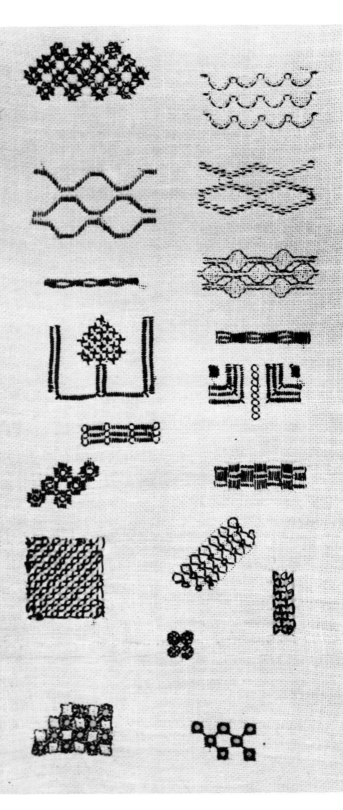

1 SQUARE STITCH

Can be used as an addition to hems (page 27). Over three threads, A–B, needle out at C. Upright back to B, slant at the back, needle out at D. Back to A and into D. Straight to C, C–E and repeat.

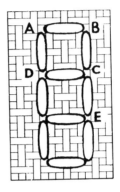
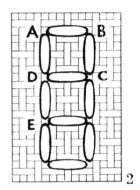

RAISED SQUARE STITCH

A–B slant at the back, needle out at D. Upright to A, needle slant at the back, out at C. C straight to B, slant at the back and out at D. Straight to C, slant at the back and into E. Repeat from A–B.

Raised Square Stitch .

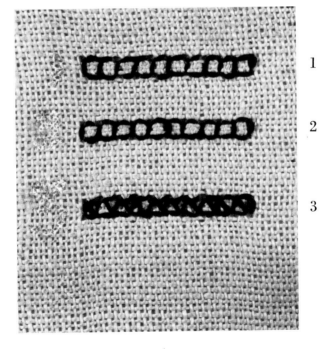

SQUARE STITCH
VARIATION

A–B needle slant from B–D on back and front. Needle in D upright to A, back to D. D–C repeat.

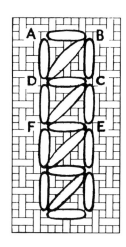

3

HEMS
See page 15

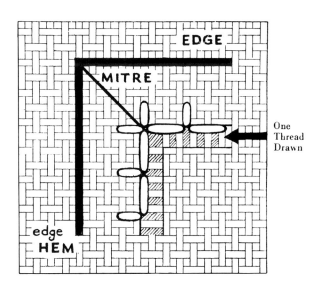

3   SQUARE DIAGONAL
WITH OPEN SPACES

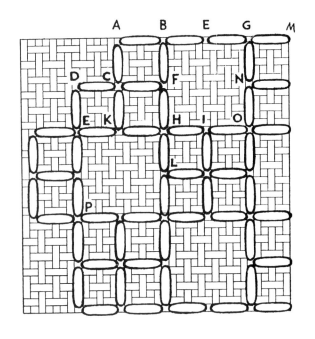

Over three threads.

First row

Needle at A–B; B–C slant at back; C–A upright; A–D slant; D–C straight; repeat.

Second row

B–E straight; E–F slant; F–B straight; B–C slant; C–F straight; F–K slant; K–C straight; C–E slant; repeat.

Third row

E–G straight; G–H over six threads, diagonally; H–F straight; F–K slant; K–H straight; H–P over six threads, diagonally; repeat.

Fourth row

G–M straight; M–N slant; N–G straight; G–H over six threads; diagonally; H–I straight; I–L slant, L–H straight; H–P over six threads diagonally; repeat from A at G.

SAMPLER 5 (*page 23*).

28

SQUARE DIAGONAL

WITH TWO THREADS LEFT

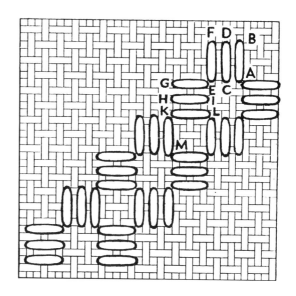

Over three threads. Needle upright A–B, C–D, E–F, F–G diagonally; G–E, H–I, K–L straight; L–M slant; repeat from A. Second row similar.

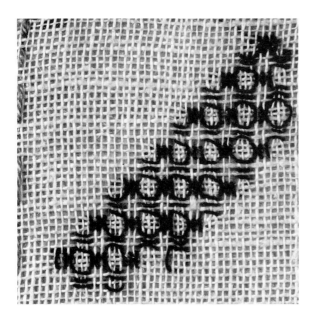

SAMPLER 25 (*page 23*)

5 SQUARE DIAGONAL

WITH SMALL SQUARES

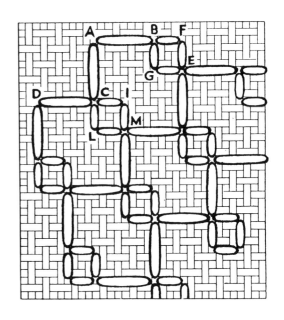

First row. Worked over four threads. Needle at A straight stitch to B; B–C diagonally; C–A upright; A D diagonally; repeat.

Second row. Worked over two threads.

Needle at E upright to F; F–G slant; G–B upright; B–M slant; M–I upright; I–L slant; L–C upright; repeat.

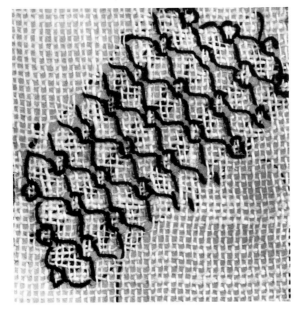

Third row. Worked over two threads.

B–F straight; F–G slant; G–E straight; E–C slant; C–I straight; I–L slant; L–M straight; repeat.

SAMPLER 49 (*page 25*)

30

SQUARE DIAGONAL

WITH BARS

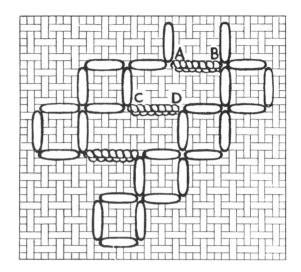

Worked over three threads. Two rows square diagonal with four threads left between. For looped bars bring needle out at A. Into B twice. Needle will be at A. Cover with loop stitches, inserting needle into C and repeat. Each bar should have the same number of loop stitches.

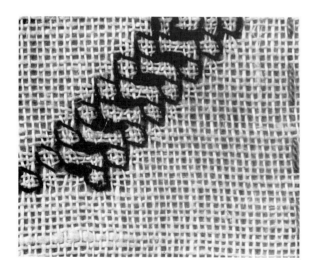

SAMPLER 27 (*page 23*)

7 BASKET STITCH

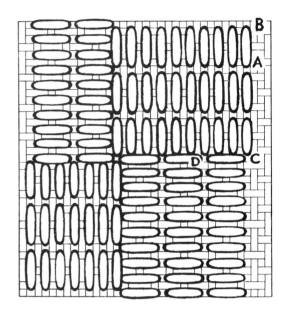

Straight stitches. Over three threads A–B ten times. Second and third rows similar.

Second detail worked at right angles to about C–D. Continue for desired size.

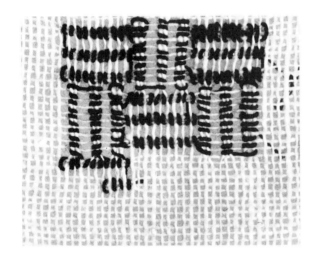

SAMPLER 10 (*page 23*)

MOSAIC STITCH

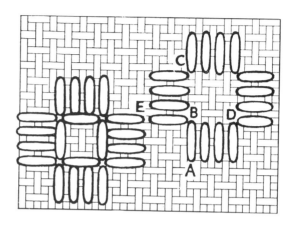

Each side has four stitches over three threads, A–B. For centre place needle at B, into C, cross at the back and bring out at D finish the square and bring needle out at E to start second detail.

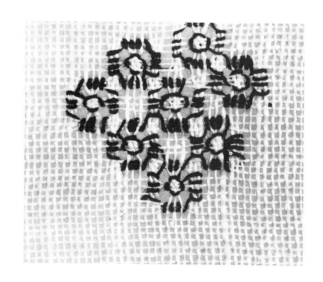

SAMPLER 46 (*page 25*)

9   PULLED CHEVRON

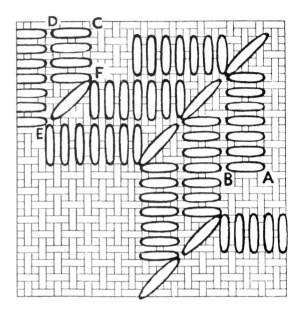

Worked over three threads. A–B seven times. Miss three threads, work one diagonal, miss three threads to form corner, work seven stitches. Work four threads at right angles to these seven, C–D; miss three, diagonal for corner, E–F, miss three, work seven. Repeat. Each row will be three threads short of previous row to allow for the diagonal

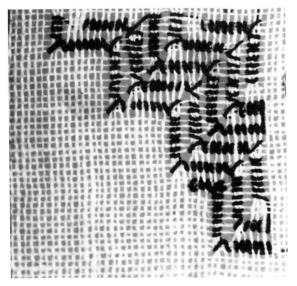

and will have three threads beyond at the other end of the row. Notice that each corner will have three stitches upright, diagonal, upright in the same hole. If a larger chevron is required use nine or eleven stitches instead of seven. These stitches are straight on the front and into next thread on the back.

SAMPLER 2 (*page 23*)

34

REVERSED DIAGONAL **10**

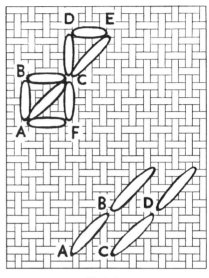

Variation

Worked from lower left- to top right-hand corners. Each straight stitch is worked twice.

Upright stitch A–B worked twice; needle diagonal A–C; needle into B, cover; B–D, needle out at C; C–D, cover; C–E repeat.

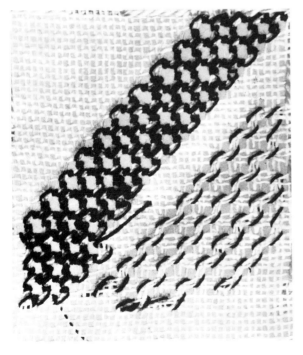

Second journey

A–F cover; repeat from A–C. Note that slanting stitches, A–C, etc., are not covered on the first journey. This covering comes on the second and subsequent journeys.

Variation

All stitches are diagonal, on the right side. Over three threads, A–B. Needle straight on the back into C. C–D diagonal, needle into B straight on the back. Repeat.

SAMPLER 12 (*page 23*)

11 SQUARE DIAGONAL

WITH ONE THREAD LEFT

Worked diagonally over three threads.

First row
Needle at A–B straight; B–C slant; C–A upright, out at D; D–E upright; E–F slant; F–D straight; D–G slant; G–H straight. Repeat.

Second row
I–M represents A–B. Repeat.

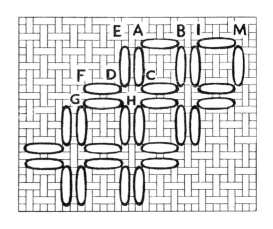

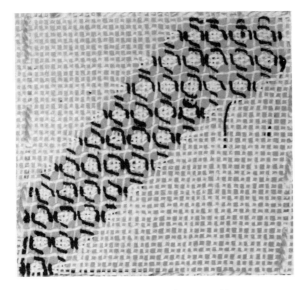

SAMPLER 13 (*page 23*)

SQUARE DIAGONAL STITCH

Worked from upper right to lower left corners. Each stitch is worked twice, needle slants on the back with second stitch.

Worked in two journeys. Upright stitch A–B, cover, needle B–C; C–A cover; A–D with needle slanting on the back, D–C, C–E. Second journey worked in the same way.

Model shows one complete row, and the same stitch used as a filling. Each row should be started at the top right-hand corner.

SQUARE DIAGONAL

WITH THREAD LEFT

Upright stitch A–B, needle slants on the back, out at C. Back into C from A, slant at the back and into D. Repeat.

Second row

Straight stitch, F–E, one thread to the right and one below A; E–G diagonally; G–F straight; F–H diagonally; repeat.

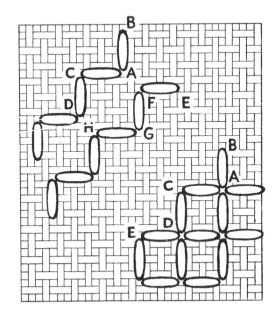

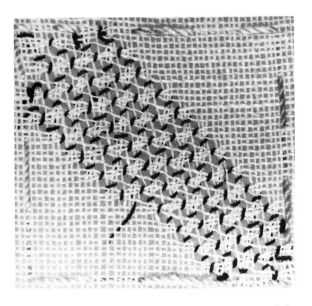

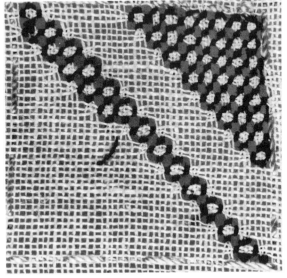

SAMPLER 14 AND 5 (*page 23*)

13 GREEK CROSS STITCH

Worked on the diagonal, from top right-hand corner. Each stitch is straight, over three threads. Four stitches, A–B, A–C, A–D, A–E, with the thread under the needle each time. Place the needle over this centre, A, and bring it out under the left-hand arm of the previous cross, F. Repeat. Do not pull this centre stitch. The holes come on the subsequent rows, where the crosses meet.

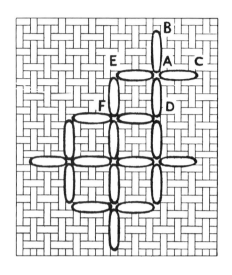

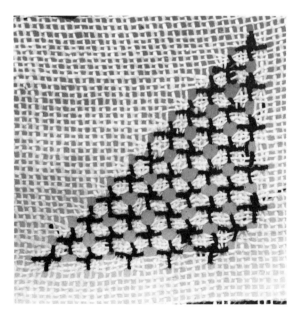

SAMPLER 15 (*page 23*)

GREEK CROSS STITCH

VARIATION

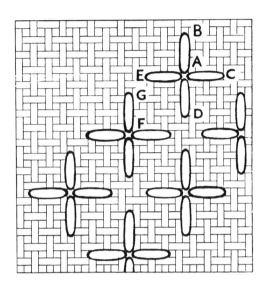

Worked as Greek cross stitch, with the second cross starting one thread to the left, and one thread underneath the first cross.

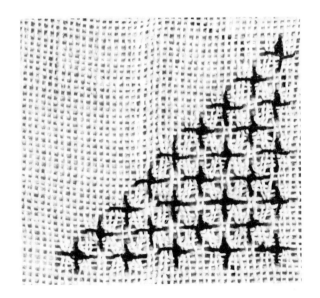

SAMPLER 22 (*page 23*)

39

15 SINGLE RAISED BAND

Worked on the diagonal, from lower left to upper right. Pick up six upright threads, A–B, place needle three threads down and three to the right C. Repeat as many rows as needed, picking up at six threads from the lowest stitch of previous row. When sufficient rows are worked these bands are covered with similar stitches to the first row, working from right to left, D–E, F–G, crossing each band.

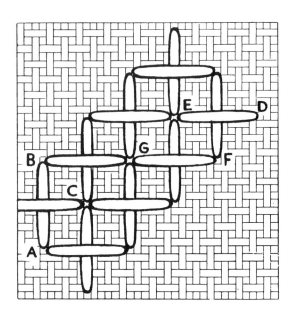

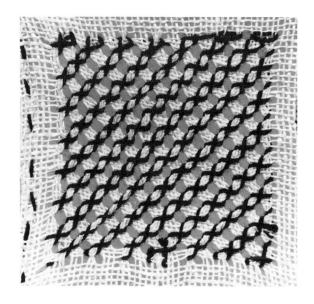

SAMPLER 48 (*page 25*)

DOUBLE RAISED BAND 16

In four journeys, over four threads. First and second rows worked as single raised band. Third and fourth rows are worked in the opposite direction, starting in the lower right hand, E–F. The first upright stitch, E–F, is eight threads from the lowest stitch in the first row. Fourth journey starts at top left hand, G–H.

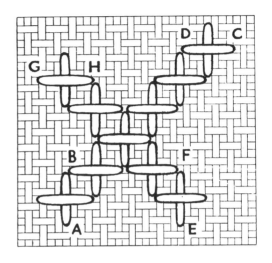

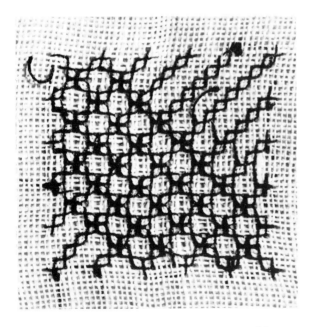

SAMPLER 28 (*page 23*)

17   SOLID EYELET

Worked over three threads, into each thread. B is the centre.

A–B, C–B, D–B, E–B (corner). Repeat round the eyelet.

SAMPLER 53 (*page 25*)

EYELET WITH SHADOW STITCH   **18**

SQUARE

For eyelet work over three threads, missing two threads after each stitch bringing needle out at A with eyelet completed.

For shadow cushion

A–C over two, out at D. D–A out at E over six threads diagonally. E upright to F and out at G. G–C upright, out at H. H–E and out at K (right corner). K–G and out at L (left corner). L–H and out at M. M–L out at N. N–F and out at O. O–M and out at D.

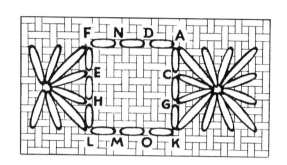

D–N and out at K. K–O and out at A, ready to commence next cushion.

These shadow stitches should be slightly pulled to give the "cushion" effect, but care must be taken not to destroy the square appearance.

SAMPLER 52 (*page 25*)

19 SINGLE EYELET STITCH

Worked diagonally from lower right-hand corner to top left. Only half the eyelet is worked on the first journey.

1. Bring needle through at arrow, and work upright stitch over three threads to A.
2. Bring needle through at B and insert again at A.
3. Bring needle through at C and return to A.
4. Bring needle through at D, three threads above and three threads to the left of A.

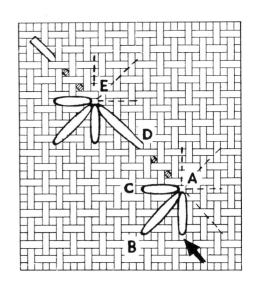

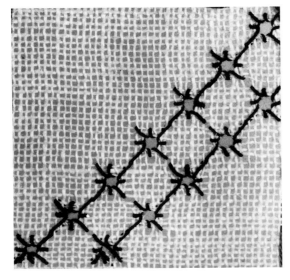

5. Work diagonal stitch from D to E, which becomes the centre of the second eyelet. This stitch is not covered at the back until the second journey. Repeat.

Second journey

Cover diagonal stitches and fill in the second side of the eyelet in the same manner as the first journey.

Always pull from the centre.

SAMPLER 23 (*page 23*)

44

Worked downwards

1. Upright stitch over six threads A to B.
2. Needle slants into C. Three threads to the right and three below B. Second time needle into B and out at A.
3. Needle slants over three threads, out at C. Second time needle out at C and into D, six threads below C.

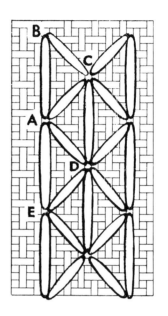

4. Needle slants over three threads into A. Second time needle into E, six threads below A.

Second row, the straight stitches are worked into the same threads as the previous rows.

SAMPLER 51 (*page 25*)

21 PULLED SATIN STITCH

VARIATION

Worked from right to left over four threads.

Six upright stitches as A–B. Six upright stitches C–D, working half-way up A–B. Six upright stitches, E–F underneath previous row. Note that these two rows pull from each other.

Repeat with long stitches under the small ones and vice versa, leaving two threads uncovered between the rows.

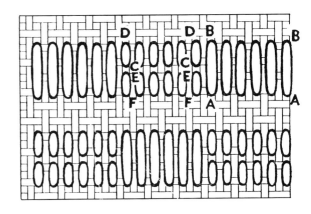

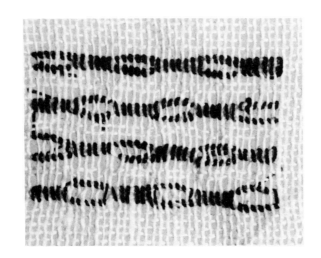

SAMPLER 40 (*page 25*)

PULLED SATIN STITCH

VARIATION

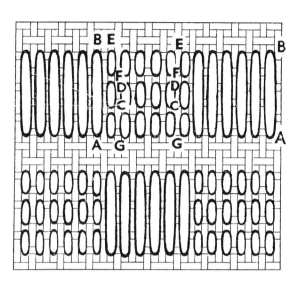

Worked from right to left over six threads.

A–B six times. Pick up the two centre threads, C–D, and work over them six times, right to left. Turn the work and make six stitches, over two, E–F, pulling from C–D. Needle out at G, work six stitches over two, G–C over two threads.

Travelling down the centre, then at the top, then lower half of these rows over two, will give the desired curve, but each row should be worked from the previous one.

There are two threads left uncovered between the subsequent rows, and the long and short stitches are reversed.

SAMPLER 43 (*page 25*)

23 PULLED BACK STITCH

Worked over three threads, downwards.

Back stitch A–B, needle into A. Needle over three A–C, back to A. Needle into D, three threads under B. Back into B, into E, three straight threads to the left. Back into D and pick-up F, cover three threads to C, back to F. Repeat.

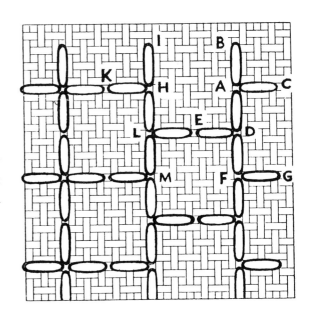

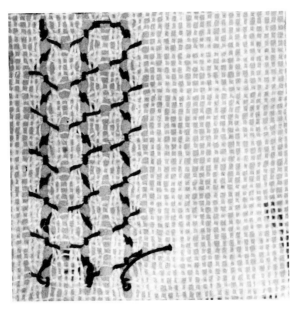

Second row

Pick up six threads from A to H, three upright into I. Back to H, needle into K, three threads to the left of H. Back into H, place needle into L, straight stitch into E, needle back to L, out at M.

Subsequent rows similar.

SAMPLER 1 (*page 23*)

48

FESTOON STITCH 24

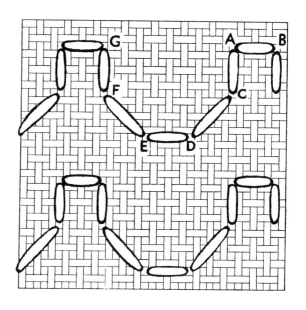

Over three threads, worked from right to left.

Pick up at A, into B, straight stitch, diagonal to C. Needle into A, diagonal into D. D–C diagonally and out at E. Straight stitch E–D, cover and needle out at F. F–E out at G. Repeat.

Subsequent rows worked alike, starting nine threads below A.

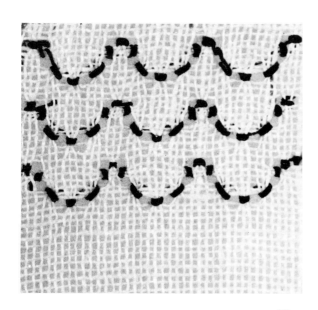

SAMPLER 37 (*page 25*)

25 EYELET STITCH FILLING

All stitches are worked twice, those round the eyelet over two threads, those into the centre are over three threads.

A–B straight, cover, A–C over three threads, needle out at D. D–A slant back to D and out at C, cover and out at E. E–D straight, cover, needle to C out at F. F–E slant,

cover, into C and out at G. G–F cover, into C needle out at H. H–G cover, needle into C out at K. K–H cover, into C out at B. B–K, cover, into C.

Subsequent eyelets touch on the straight stitches, leaving a blank square between the diagonal stitches.

SAMPLER 50 (*page 25*)

ROSETTE STITCH 26

Worked diagonally, over three threads. A–B with needle diagonally to C; C–A needle out at D; straight to E, diagonally to F; F–D needle out at G; G–H, needle out at K; K–H, out at M; M–O, back to M; M–N out at A. Cross stitch in each space. A–N; M–B; K–A; C–H; G–D; F–H; D–O; M–E. Needle to H and make a square stitch round the centre, crossing the stitches on the back.

Second rosette will start three threads diagonally from K–H.

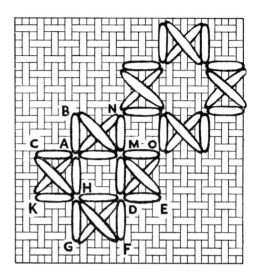

SAMPLER 36 (*page 25*)

27   RINGED BACK STITCH

Worked in two journeys over three threads, from right to left. First journey work upper part of the first ring, then lower part of second ring, repeat. Second journey work the reverse way. Three upright stitches A–B, needle in A, diagonally into C; C–B needle out at D. D–C, cover with needle out at E. E–F and needle out at G. G–F, cover with needle out at H. H–G straight, cover with needle out at I. Repeat as from A–B.

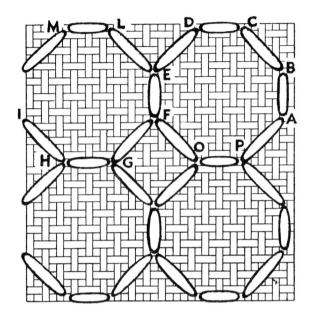

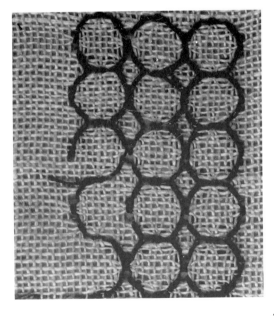

Second journey to complete the ring A–B, out at P. P–A diagonally with needle out at O. O–P straight, cover with needle out at F. F–O cover, with needle out at E. E–F with needle out at L, repeat as from B–C.

Note that the upright stitches, F–E etc., are not covered on the first journey. The covering stitch here comes on the subsequent rows.

SAMPLER 20 (*page 23*)

RINGED BACK STITCH

WITH BOX

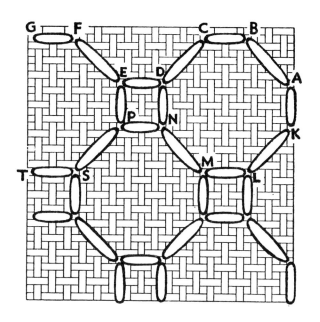

Worked over three threads in two journeys, from right to left.

First row

Needle up at A, into B diagonally, back to A, across to C. C–B straight, back to B, diagonally to D. Cover D–C, place needle in E. Straight stitch E–D, cover with needle to D, across to F. F–E, needle across to G. Straight stitch G–F, repeat from C–B.

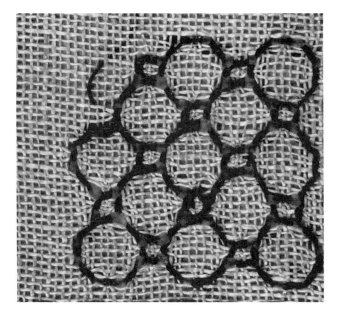

Second row

K–A upright, cover, A–L diagonally. L–K, cover with needle out at M. M–L straight, cover with needle diagonally into N. N–M and back to N. N–D straight, cover with needle into P. P–N twice P–E cover with needle into S, three diagonal from P. S–T straight, cover. Repeat. Model shows one row unfinished.

SAMPLER 6 (*page 23*)

29 HONEYCOMB STITCH

1. Bring needle through at arrow and work straight stitch over three threads to right, inserting at A.
2. Bring needle through at B and work upright stitch into A, bring needle through at B again.
3. Insert needle at C, making straight stitch over three threads to left.
4. With needle in upright position bring through at D, and again insert at C, bringing it through at D.

   Repeat this for length required.

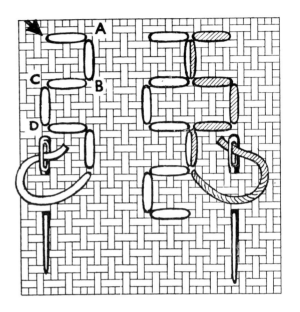

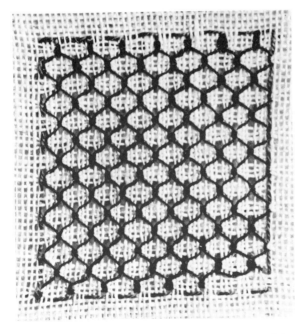

Second journey

Bring needle through three threads to the right of A and work straight stitch into A.

Then proceed as shown by shaded line in diagram.

SAMPLER 16 (*page 23*)

54

VARIATION

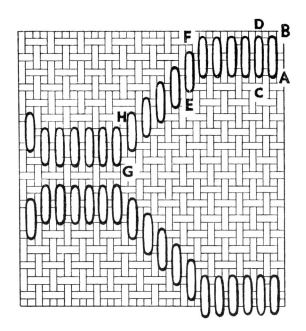

Worked from right to left. Six upright stitches over three threads A–B C–D. Five upright stitches, each stitch is one thread lower than the previous stitch, F–E.

Repeat six upright stitches G–H.

Six upright stitches, each stitch one thread higher than the previous row.

Second row worked the same, with one thread left uncovered at the straight row and travelling the opposite way.

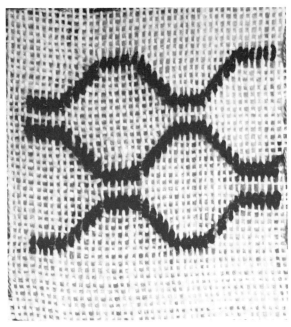

SAMPLER 38 (*page 25*)

31 LOZENGE STITCH

VARIATION

Worked from right to left. Pick up three threads at A, needle into B crossing at the back into C. Insert at D and place needle at E, one thread above and three threads to left of C.

Pick up three threads, needle into F, two threads below E and insert at G. Repeat until there are five downward stitches, continue in the same way, travelling upwards.

Second row worked the same, two threads lower; at centre row. Both these Lozenge stitches look better if worked over two threads.

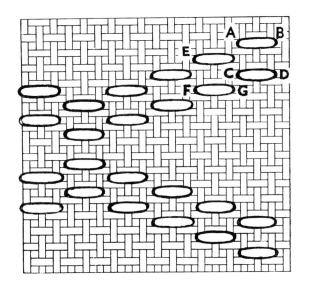

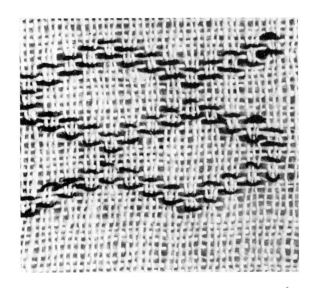

SAMPLER 39 (*page 25*)

BRAID STITCH

OVER TWO THREADS

32

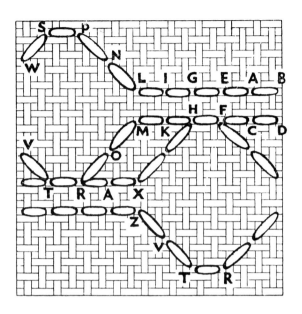

Worked from right to left, over two threads. Needle in at A, into B, slant to C.

Into D, out at E. Continue until there are four back stitches. Needle in M to make the fifth back stitch, into K, out at L and into I, diagonally to N, two to left and two above L. N–L and out at O. O–M out at P. P diagonally to N and out at R.

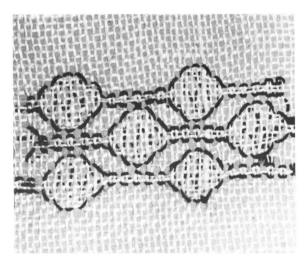

R–O and out at S. S straight to P, diagonally into T. T straight to R, out at W. W–S out at V. V–T and out two diagonally and two to left of W. Into W, needle out two above and two to left of V. Repeat from A–B which will be the same as A–X.

SAMPLER 41 (*page 25*)

33 WAVE STITCH

Worked on the straight, each stitch is worked twice.

Pick up three threads diagonally, A–B, from right to left. Needle back to A, pick up six threads horizontally, needle at C. Needle back to B, cover, pick up six threads horizontally to D. Repeat. Second row worked the same, with stitches the reverse way.

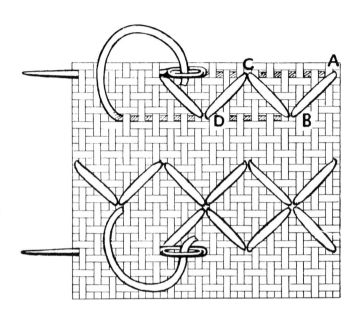

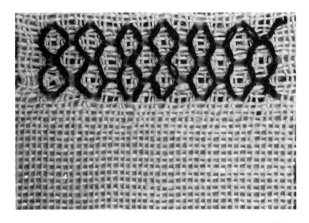

WAVE STITCH

VARIATION

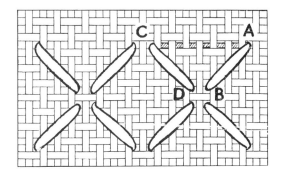

Worked as Wave stitch, with one thread left uncovered between each diagonal stitch. There will be seven threads picked up on the straight instead of six.

35 PULLED SQUARE

Straight stitches over three threads, start in the centre A–B. Miss three threads to form corner, second and subsequent rows are worked into the last hole of the previous rows, the three stitches, two straight and one diagonal, which form the corner may be omitted and the corners left bare, but threads must be left to make a right-angle turn. These squares should not be more than $1\frac{1}{2}$ inches in diameter.

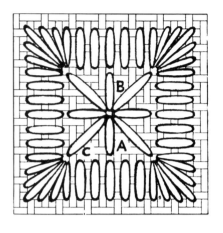

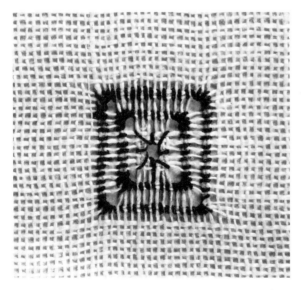

SAMPLER 4 (*page 23*)

PULLED SQUARE

VARIATION

Same method of work as above but with one thread left uncovered between each row. There will be four threads left in the centre on each side.

SAMPLER 32 (*page 23*)

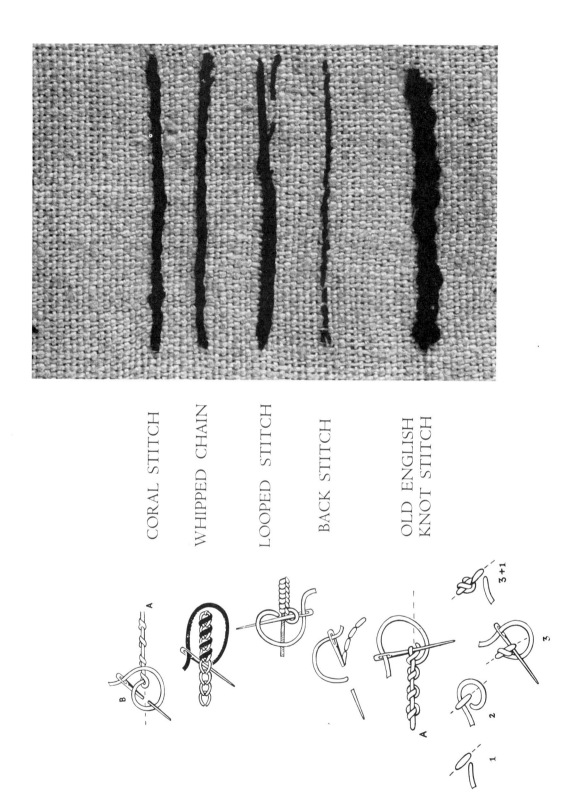

CORAL STITCH

WHIPPED CHAIN

LOOPED STITCH

BACK STITCH

OLD ENGLISH
KNOT STITCH

OUTLINES FOR USING WITH PULLED FILLINGS

For the geometrical type the square diagonal and the square stitches are the most suitable, though a small satin stitch will answer the purpose. When the design is a free-hand one there is more scope, and the outlines can be varied, in size as well as in the type. The models will show the various weights of the stitches, and of course, these can be varied by the thread used. A hard thread is advisable.

1. *Coral Stitch*
   Needle up at A, thread is kept in place by holding it with the thumb of the left hand, needle is placed under this thread at B and the thread comes under the needle, as in loop stitch, and is then pulled. When pulling this thread bring the needle upright, not towards you, this will make the knot firm and even.

2. *Whipped Chain.*
   Needle out at A, place it back into A with the thread looped under the needle and into B. Continue and then whip over the two edges of the chain, C–D. This will make a rope-like outline.

3. *Looped Stitch.*
   A thread is laid first and then small tight loop stitches are worked over the laid stitch, picking up a small stitch on the material. This can be a very tight solid outline.

4. *Back Stitch.*
   Worked either in a thin or heavy thread.

5. *Old English Knot,* also known as *Palestrina Knot.*
   This knot is usually worked in a heavy thread. Bring needle up to A and make a small stitch 1. Slip needle through this stitch from right to left 2. Needle is slipped from right to left under the lower end of 1. This stitch, 3, has the thread under the needle as in loop stitch and it should not be pulled too tight.

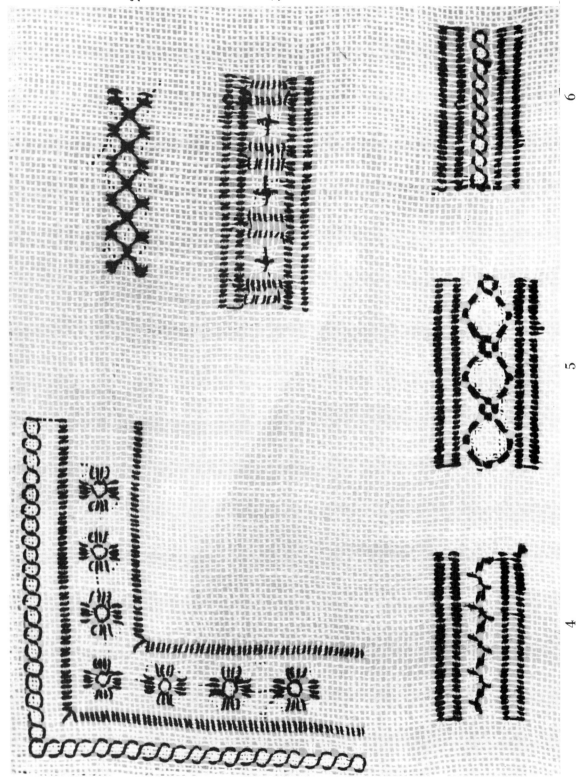

BORDERS

1. One row of raised square stitch (which could be used for each border). One row pulled satin stitch. Leave eleven threads and repeat this row. In the centre of these two rows, work details of mosaic stitch, three threads apart and one thread uncovered at top and lower edges.

2. Worked in three rows. Over three threads work three pulled satin stitches, leave four threads and repeat. The second and third rows are worked in a similar way, the first stitch comes into the last one of the previous row. The thread is then fastened on under the last group of the first row and is carried under the last group of the second row. This is repeated on the last row.

3. Two rows of pulled satin stitch touching each other. Two rows of pulled satin stitch six times at right angles, leave six threads and repeat. In this space work one detail of Greek cross stitch.

4. Border as 3 with one row of pulled back stitch in the centre.

5. Border as 3 and 4 with one row of ringed back stitch in centre.

6. Border as 3 and 4. One thread left uncovered at each side with one row of raised square stitch in the centre.

All these borders are worked over three threads in the models.

GEOMETRICAL SATIN STITCH

Worked from right to left. To fasten on, run the thread from left to right, taking care that this thread does not interfere with the working thread, in other words, this fastening on should be in the centre of the satin stitches. To fasten off, run the thread through the design on the back, with a small back stitch to keep it firm. Always keep the needle straight on the front, with a slant on the back. Even tension and a thread which entirely covers the material are the main points in this stitch.

Model 1

Worked in four sections. Work twice over 2, 4, 6, 8, threads, then reverse, twice over 8, 6, 4, 2. The second section is worked the same the stitches joining diagonally. There are two threads left uncovered between the sections.

If required in a larger size, work over three threads and into groups of 3, 6, 9, 12.

Model 2

Diagonal squares. Each stitch is worked on the diagonal, over 1, 3, 5, 7, 5, 3, 1, the next square travels the opposite way. After four of these squares are worked, an eyelet is worked in the centre with one thread left uncovered.

Model 3

A damask filling. Worked over 2, 4, 6, 4, 2. The 2 is not repeated. Second and subsequent rows. One thread left uncovered and the stitch over 2 comes directly under the 6 of the previous row.

Model 4. A border.

Work over 2, 3, 4, 5, 6, 7, 6, 5, 4, 3, 2. Repeat omitting the second 2. Second row. Worked with the same numbers but with the long stitch opposite the small one. A row of raised square stitch on either side will form a good border.

GEOMETRICAL SATIN STITCH

Model 5

Work 3 times over three threads, then 3 times over six, keeping a level edge.

Model 6

Work over 2, 4, 6, 8, 6, 4, 2 threads. Do not repeat the 2. Now work a second row, exactly like the first, and work an eyelet into the spaces between the two rows. To work these eyelets work round the lower half in the first space, into the upper half of the second space, reversing on the return journey. The last spoke of the eyelet will not be covered until the second journey.

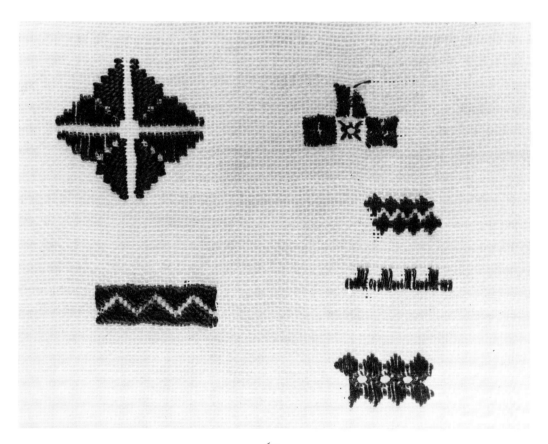

DOUBLE RUNNING
OR HOLBEIN STITCH

This design (p. 69) was adapted from a painting by Hans Holbein of the hands of Lady Jane Seymour (the mother of King Edward VI). It is shown as a frill on the cuff of her sleeve. It was reproduced in the "Agricultural Gazette" in this country in 1851. Miss Lovell has used one strand of black filoselle on white scrim, working over two threads. It is interesting to note that all the stitches are straight ones. (*Worked by Miss Valerie Lovell, Winchester.*)

INDEX

Back stitch, 63
  pulled, 22, 23, 48
  ringed, 22, 23, 52, 53
Band, raised, 22, 23
  double, 41
  single, 24, 25, 40
Basket stitch, 22, 23, 32
Bisso linen, 20
Black work fillings, 16
Borders, 15, 65
  satin stitch, 22, 23
Braid stitch, 24, 25, 57
Buttonholing stitch, 11

Cameron, Mrs., 19
  samplers by, 69; *Frontispiece*
Campbell, Etta, *Linen Embroideries*, 20, 22, 23
C.B. threads, 21
Chain stitch, whipped, 62, 63
Chevron stitch, pulled, 22, 23, 34
Christie, Mrs., *Samplers and Stitches*, 20
Colour, use of, 12
Coral stitch, 62, 63
Croft, Miss M., 20

Damask filling, 22, 23, 66
Day, Lewis, F., *Art in Needlework* (quoted), 11
Diagonal stitch, reversed, 22, 23
  square, 22–25, 28–31, 36, 37
D.M.C. coton perle, 16, 18, 20
  Encyclopaedia of Needlework, 20
Double raised band, 41
  running stitch, 16, 22, 23, 68, 69

Egyptian embroidery, 16
Embroiderers Guild, The, 20
English Knot stitch, Old, 62
Eyelet, 22–25
  filling stitch, 50
  stitch, single, 44
  stitch, solid, 24, 25, 42
  with shadow stitch, 24, 25, 43
Eyestrain, avoidance of, 12

Fastening on and off, 14
Festoon stitch, 24, 25, 49

Geometrical satin stitch, 64, 66, 67
Glamis linen, 18, 20
Glenshee linen, 16, 20
Greek cross stitch, 22–25, 38, 39

Hems, 14
Holbein stitch, 16, 68, 69
Honeycomb stitch, 22, 23, 54

Interlacing stitches, 11
Italian linen, 21

Knot stitch, Old English, 62
Knotting stitches, 11
Knox L.C. threads, 20

Linens, 12, 20
Lofthouse, Kate, *Drawn Fabric*, 20
Looped stitch, 22, 23, 62, 63
Lozenge stitch, 24, 25, 55, 56
Lovell, Miss, 17, 68

Mosaic stitch, 24, 25, 35

Needles, 13, 21

Old English Knot stitch, 62, 63
Outlines, 63
Oversewing stitch, 11

Palestrina Knot stitch, 63
Pesel, Miss L. F., *Historical Designs for Embroidery*, 19, 20
Plummer Ltd., Winchester, 20
Pouncing, 13
Pressing and stretching finished work, 17
Pricking, 13
Pulled back stitch, 22, 23, 48
  chevron stitch, 22, 23, 34
  fillings, outlines for use with, 63
  satin stitch, 22–25, 46, 47
  square stitch, 22, 23, 60, 61

Quilting 12

Raised band stitch, 22, 23
  double, 41
  single, 24, 25, 40
Raised square stitch, 22–25
Reversed diagonal, 22, 23
Ringed back stitch, 22, 23, 52, 53
Rosette stitch, 24, 25, 51
Running stitch, 11
  double, 16, 22, 23

Samplers, 18, 22–61, 69; *Frontispiece*
Satin stitch, 22, 23
  geometrical, 64, 66, 67
  pulled, 22–25, 46, 47
Scrim, 20
Seward, Mrs., 20
Shadow stitch, solid eyelet with, 24, 25, 43
Single raised band, 22–25, 40
Smocks, 12
Solid eyelet stitch, 24, 25, 42
Square diagonal stitch, 22–25, 28–31, 36, 37
Square stitch, 24, 25, 26, 27
  pulled, 22, 23, 60, 61
Stitches:
  Back, 63
  Basket, 22, 23, 32
  Braid, 24, 25, 57
  Buttonholing, 11
  Coral, 62, 63
  Eyelet filling, 50
    single, 44
    solid, 24, 25, 42
    with shadow stitch, 24, 25, 42
  Festoon, 49
  Geometrical satin, 64, 66, 67
  Greek cross, 22–25, 38, 39

Holbein, 16, 68, 69
Honeycomb, 22, 23, 54
Interlacing, 11
Knotting, 11, 62
Looped, 22, 23, 62, 63
Lozenge, 24, 25, 55, 56
Mosaic, 24, 25, 35
Old English Knot, 62, 63
Oversewing, 11
Palestrina Knot, 63
Pulled back, 22. 23, 48
  chevron, 22, 23, 34
  satin, 22–25, 46, 47
  square, 22, 23, 60, 61
Raised band, 22–25, 40, 41
Reversed diagonal, 35
Ringed back, 22, 23, 52, 53
Rosette, 24, 25, 51
Running, 11, 16, 22, 23
Satin, 22–25, 46, 47, 64–67
Square, 24–27
  diagonal, 22–25, 28–31, 36, 37
Stroke, 16
Three-sided, 24, 25, 45
Wave, 22, 23, 58, 59
Whipped chain, 62, 63
Stretching and pressing finished work, 17
Stroke stitch, 16

Tension, 13
Thomas, Mary, *Dictionary of Stitches*, 20
Threads, 13, 20, 21
Three-sided stitch, 24, 25, 45
Transferring design to material, 13
Transfers, 13, 20

Wave stitch, 22, 23, 58, 59
Whipped chain stitch, 62, 63